# In the Land We Imagined Ourselves

## Books by Jonathan Johnson

Poetry

*Mastodon, 80% Complete*
*In the Land We Imagined Ourselves*

Nonfiction

*Hannah and the Mountain*

# In the Land We Imagined Ourselves

## Jonathan Johnson

**Carnegie Mellon University Press**
Pittsburgh 2010

## Acknowledgments

Grateful acknowledgment is made to the editors of the magazines and anthologies in which these poems, or versions of them, first appeared:

*Ascent*: "Getting Further from the Idaho Line," "Parole," "The First Thing You Knew of Nothing"; *Epoch*: "She of Tioga Creek"; *Cream City Review*: "Public Relations Pastoral"; *Hayden's Ferry Review*: "The Big Drop Is the Only Way Home," "Fire Season"; *LitRag*: "Snow Moving Like Fire"; *North American Review*: "Vango's, Tuesday Night in the Week of the Buddha's Enlightenment"; *Passages North*: "Please," "In"; *Ploughshares*: "Influence"; *Prairie Schooner*: "Pitch," "Resolve"; *ReDivider*: "The Spotting Scope"; *Seattle Review*: "Bones in the River"; *Southern Review*: "Perspective Unrecovered"; *Third Coast*: "Brave Coast, No Wheels," "Original Sins and Cover Tunes"; *Quarterly West*: "Geological Proportions."

"Surplus" and "Three Cafés" appeared in *The Long Journey: Pacific Northwest Poets* (Oregon State University Press, 2006).

"Three Cafés," "None of This Is Saying Goodbye," "Perspective Unrecovered," "Pitch," and "The Word 'Curl'" appeared in *Poetry Thirty: Thirty Something Thirty-Something American Poets* (Mammoth Books, 2005).

The publication of this book is made possible by a grant from the Pennsylvania Council on the Arts.

Book design by Graeme Ross-Munro

PENNSYLVANIA
COUNCIL
ON THE
ARTS

# Contents

Prelude                                                          9

I

Wonderful                                                       13
Original Sins and Cover Tunes                                   14
Solitude                                                        16
New You, New Me                                                 18
Postcard with Black Rocks                                       20
The First Thing You Knew of Nothing                             21
Please                                                          22

II

The Big Drop Is the Only Way Home                               25
Public Relations Pastoral                                       27
Snow Moving Like Fire                                           28
Richard's Thermos                                               30
Pitch                                                           32
Getting Further from the Idaho Line                             33
After I Left                                                    34
Parole                                                          35
Night Bicycle                                                   36
Geological Proportions                                          38

III

American Ballad                                                 43

IV

She of Tioga Creek                                      53
Three Cafés                                             54
Influence                                               56
University Surplus                                      57
Bones in the River                                      59
The Spotting Scope                                      60
Fire Season                                             61
Brave Coast, No Wheels                                  63

V

Perspective Unrecovered                                 67
The Word "Curl"                                         69
Tend                                                    70
Flanigan's Pen                                          71
Third Street and the Stolen Boat                        73
Leave and the Dream of This Street Starts Over          76

VI

Detail                                                  79
Daughter                                                80
In                                                      81
None of This Is Saying Goodbye                          83
Resolve                                                 84
Morning in a New Year                                   85
Teleological North: Year's End                          86
Vango's, Tuesday Night in the
        Week of the Buddha's Enlightenment              87

*"yes, in spite of all"*

—John Keats

for Russell Thorburn

There is a tree I've imagined.
It's big and solitary, but not stately,
just itself in the snow, bare against gray sky.
It branches out to the end of itself.
It is not a tree I've seen but is particular.
That is, I'd know it if I noticed it.
And if, walking at the end of the year,
I saw the tree I've imagined,
I would no longer be me.

I

## Wonderful

He had an audience
and something specific to pray.
Tuesdays, Thursdays and Saturdays he could
take the stairs up to Dialysis two
at a time to tell her the temperature,
the sun or seagull, waves or no waves.

She listened while he worked his descriptions
and wanted how he and no one else saw.
And now the drama of this tight corner
a block off a different body of water—
delivery trucks, moped, mini-excavator trenching a line,
the turn too narrow for this Peugeot van,
and now *Policía Local* with his ticket book,
all in the space of a small stage adjacent to his café table—
will go unknown, along with the pots of flowers
hung from the wrought iron as if overlooking it all
and with names she would have known.

## Original Sins and Cover Tunes

When he solos my friend watches his hands
work the same drowsy precision they'd get
when he was drinking and those fingers knew
every fret's home and every note's name.
What's taking his muscles takes years.  Meanwhile
he's sober.  His wife comes to listen.
He wears sandals and goes home when it's done.
But believe his foreboding when he says
*train's comin'* in his "Talking MD Blues."
It's for you.  He's already given up
the closing time bike down to the park
where he'd sleep his drunk into the sound of waves.

He rode that red bike across his thirties,
wrote songs starring the regulars in Ten o'Clock's,
made a case for himself saying your name
into the mic when you walked in mid-song.
But Ten o'Clock's is now an organic foods
art on the walls red wine professors' restaurant
that closes at nine.  Sunday Mass he sits
on a folding chair to play rock and roll
with his son's youth band.  He rises for work

before dawn.  But every few months he'll
set up a Friday gig at this corner pub
and somewhere in the second set find his
motorcycle with a short in the headlight,
sight flickering out for a few seconds
now and then in the Egyptian night,
a lion once *there in the road and then gone,*
the Black Hills out a bus window, a girl
offering to follow him to Africa.

A few days after the diagnosis
his daughter came crying to his office,

ashamed of such selfishness, but
did he know, would this happen to her too?
His bike knees lasted the summer, so he biked
everywhere.  There was one more year of streetlights'
drunk company, singing hoarse and angry,
steamed mussels and Corona at lunch hour,
the salty sweet buttered world of everything,
everything that would be taken away.

*Train's comin'* he says and the guitar agrees
so softly it must mean all of us.  The door's
propped open.  We can smell waves five blocks away.

## Solitude

It's good to see you too,
but if you're like me there's a field in your head
and if you could be there—
finch song and quiver of hot air between here
and horizon, satin iridescence of sun
on the surface of barley when you wade in—
you'd for once be done with all the bewildered desire
that floods into conversations like this,
when it's been as long as it's been
and the certainty of being exactly you
is a yanked tooth.

In these hours you crowd with faces
there's an underriding silence of dirt, turned months ago
and baked in clods that crumble to dust
and the smallest pebbles
when you stoop and squeeze them between your fingers.
Somewhere where no one is asking questions.

Or, maybe you walk every so often
down beaches of anonymity.
Maybe you've sat on a rise
where dune grass takes its first hold on sand.
Maybe every wave tips forward, arrives, and is new.
Knowing your depthless goodness, if you're like me,
you expect the same for you.

If you're like me, we'll stand here awhile,
doing what we do. *Oh fine. How 'bout you?*
If you could keep yourself from speaking,
you'd still be spoken to.
But when a mess of tree swallows leaves a tree,
turns left and swoops low over that field of yours,

it's unrehearsed.  You at your best.
Imagination on the loose.  My restless voice replaced
and your restless voice replaced
by sky darkening to a pure eternity
you've never, through all these weary years,
let yourself forget.

## New You, New Me

Who I was jumps a mountain bike off a north coast college
      town curb and cuts across slow, end of summer traffic,
he sits under the 6 A.M. fade of aurora to dawn, the last one
      awake beside the beach fire,
he's halfway down Mexico to Belize in a saggy-spring
      Cutlass Sierra,
he dances through trumpet blast with the waitress while the
      middle-aged divorced guys chew their straws,
wakes in her twin bed, a half empty bottle of Bass on the
      nightstand beside them,
wears Hawaiian shirts and walks the biggest shaggy dog
      anyone's ever seen,
he can quote lines of Buber on kindness from memory,
he strings a necklace of driftwood and gull feathers to hang
      from his rearview mirror
and gets word his poem about standing at the window in
      Keats' Roman casa's been taken.
Oh my daughter, your father was good at a good time.
Happy to be hungry in the oh so cinematic air.
May you too know singing along with the windows down,
      air through your hair, and the blossoming conviction
      that someone should be getting this on film.
At two you already know your audience,
standing on your café chair to dance the Cookie Dance for
      your reflection in the window.
Bent to see your feet walk their slow, deliberate walk down
      the hall,
you pause midway across the stage of the bathroom door I've
      left open, glance up at me and say, "Anya passing by."
And so we all are and so you'll learn,
each of us passing as we take more or less notice of one
      another's shirts,

the cookie or waitress we're dancing with,
the timeless profundity of what we read and remember
and say.
Mostly though, it's our later selves we're singing to,
the camera of expected recollection that pans the Tuscan hills
to find us gazing across the pearly-green middle
distance of this one undergraduate August.
Go ahead, make yourself a self you'll be nostalgic for,
and may someone come and rescue you
the way you rescued me, on the pillow beside you telling
my story,
when your eyes split me open
and your hand reached over to touch my speaking lips.

## Postcard with Black Rocks

The photo was taken some time ago.
I've seen it on the wire racks at Jack's IGA
for a few years at least.  But on a day
she was doing what? Sunny as it was did she notice
the search party of stratocumuli
crossing over?  No recalling the impossibly lost
name of when the lens opened
on spray where some jetty met the wave,
where the wave went on
to the pebble cove beach
where I've stood, handful of ash
and a yellowish bit of bone
in daylight for the first time now.
No guessing if she'd chosen that place
by the day in the photo.  In the photo
nature is dateless.  Another breaker out there
always on the way in.  No copyright
on the other side.  We don't get them back,
she'd say of the days.  There's some chance
she was there for that one,
if not at the moment of composition, not
actually parked in the pull-out behind a figure
at the tripod then maybe later (the color's
bright as morning) and if so there's a chance
I was there too and both our windows were down.
Certainly, she still had days,
an abundance of days, that day of the photo,
to go there, or anywhere, even the parking lot at IGA
to wait and watch the searching clouds and cars pass
while I went in. . . . Now I walk to the place
in the postcard alone, though not right now.
Not today I mean.  It's winter there today.
And it's night.  It looks nothing like this.

## The First Thing You Knew of Nothing

The first thing you knew of nothing
was not the buzz above the young undertaker's ears.
The first thing you knew of nothing was,
I suppose, my saying I love you
again and again.  Or maybe my hand
on your cheek the moment it quit feeling.
But that I let him take you from that bed,
roll you away from your snowed-over garden,
your window, your bare trees without us
is the first of the things for which I
can never apologize.  We'd left by then,
on someone's instructions.
You can never again say, "Don't be silly."
And you do not know where we went
to while, to kill, to keep the time,
though you'd eaten there often
and would (as they say) be glad.
Off and on all morning a trapezoid of light
lit the wall.  I cannot ask, "Could you see it
beyond what you saw of my face?"
If you surmised the overcast would break
you do not know how right you were.
Never mind.  I can say nothing
of the sun that shone all afternoon.
Or how it began the world you'd wished
us into, from which we cannot
deliver our ever-lengthening report.

## Please

If I arrive at the gate, spent pen
in my shirt pocket, hands full of leaves
to return, the park will take me back,
no questions asked.  So the park's existence
is a little like you living on.

There's a day, four or five months off.
Far down in February's dry wind twinkling cold red
radio towered horizon it waits,
rehearsing its warm breeze for my short sleeves,
readying sun for eyelids I'll close in your backyard.

I stand watching children
until the bell calls them in then watch the swing
swinging on a little after they're gone.
I have time to keep standing here.
I have time for you.

II

## The Big Drop Is the Only Way Home
#### —Capt. Joe W. Kittinger


To the not unending narration of what's happened
around me I add another aurora borealis, this one
wind rising ice white off black ridged horizon
over head and highway between Glasgow and Wolf Point
as the U-Haul's hazards pulse like hypothesis, red and small
on the gravel shoulder where I parked and left it
to wade into dark ocean of unfenced prairie
these few hundred feet closer to the northern sky.
Forgive me for making this case of a durable history
so current.  Don't we all want a little revelation, *America's*
                *Moving Adventure*
our private reinvention as flames form in mid-air
and consume our stories?  Must we settle for revision?
Ink out the U-Haul, the Dakota atop its flatbed trailer,
our old 4Runner idling behind (Amy and Yukon inside
with the heater on and aurora through windshield, thanks
                anyway)
and it's ten thousand years ago.  Or ten minutes. Or any era
the aurora streamed its dusty streamers of cathedral light
without us.  But like wagontrainers we carry
the day into night against our own rebirth
because we can't bear to die away from it:
the bed we know each other by; the boots and brass
                candelabrum;
basil sprouting in terra cotta; end tables and sweatshirts
bearing in dresser-drawered blindness our allegiances
to certain universities while another day strains against its line
like Yukon out the door of Room 14, La Casa Motel,
and into the low dawn of Glasgow's dewy scents
across U.S. 2 and through trackside weedlots
under elevators of grain and expectation, airwaves
full of futures and *GOOD LUCK SCOTTIES!  HOMECOMING*
                *1999*
on a banner over the end of town.

Even in the great everpresence of eastern Montana it seems
the future's for all of us and we're for the future.
Which we pair up with the past the way we make
the Homecoming Queen slow dance with the King
because they make a cute couple: Glasgow, Montana;
Norwich, North Dakota; Dover, Idaho.
Though her taffetaed waist feels nice in his hands,
she isn't his, and outside the spotlight her boyfriend
fingers his tie and looks at his shoes.
And the U-Haul we rented one-way from Waynesburg, PA
says FLORIDA on its side under a six-foot space shuttle,
solid rocket boosters presumably full as these Glasgow silos
and ready to *go!* We've certainly gone, pulled
the Dakota across its namesake as the 4Runner followed.
Capt. Joe W. Kittinger went to twenty and one-half miles
in his balloon, stepped from the gondola
into an August day, 1960, arms open to the drop
of water and cloud curve below, and *No wind*
*whistles or billows my clothing.* Here. Eighty miles under the
            aurora.
Where this weightlessness is also an illusion. The dazzle of
            ascension
after days of driving. A few minutes without motion.
Up the road I'll look back. Up the road at La Casa Motel
I'll read Kittinger's words from the National Geographic on
            the nightstand.
*Then I roll over on my back and find an eerie sight.*
*The white balloon contrasts starkly with a sky as black as night.*
Up the road. Up the road. I'll lighten my load.
Up the road at the edge of Glasgow I'll know
that a Fabulous Hudson Hornet floats on blocks over a field
of frosted purple blossomed knapweed behind a Pizza Hut
and the glint that still flashes off its baked chrome
comes down from the sky that takes us all.

## Public Relations Pastoral

She wants him in the smell of doug fir on his shirt.
He wants to be wanted this way,
has worn his boots and rolled his sleeves
and wouldn't go near that Karaoke microphone
for ten times the fifty dollars cash prize
though he does know some Johnny Cash and older R.E.M.
by heart and taps his boot toe almost imperceptibly
on the brass boot rail as he leans in to order
himself another, and what is she drinking?

Our approval is of no consequence so you needn't bother
with the reprimand when I say she plans
how she'll please him crawling up his not-quite-composed
        torso
and giving him a drowsy smile,
when she'll pull the pin from her hair and let its fragments fall
in his face because she's reminded how soft her hair is
tucking a loose wisp behind her ear
to hear him say something funny
about his family's unfixable but lovable tractor
eternally stranded in the far field,
how they harvest around it
and the uncut alfalfa flowers above the axles.

She imagines herself in a floral skirt at a long outdoor table,
pouring and passing the wine.

And you ride your booth into the easy night
where even the salmon above the bar is amateur,
stunned and agape and leaping
over the glistening colors of liquor
as you participate in the faceless voices spilling over you,
her hand on top of his.

## Snow Moving Like Fire

Over fir boughs
of mountain crest
blowing a wave
over moon until moon
is no guide and no god

and the spruce
are directionless arrows
obliterated and flaring
to the canyon

that clears night
into cloud swirl
mountainless air
of blizzard black soldiers

climbing blinded
by the churn
of a rage not their own
and an enduring rip
of wind that began

as granite the glacial
striations and larkspur
and the blood
in the bull moose's
urine stain on old snow

already obscured
by the first new flakes
and to be dark far
under the drifts of morning
comes meanwhile

twenty miles off and
five thousand feet down
where I stand
to the plate glass storm
that's mere rain this low

and stare
snug and certain
into the end
of what every one
of us will see.

## Richard's Thermos


Well we were way up way way up
snow in July kind of up there
building road with Ligans MacInry
driving a big old D-7
and you're supposed to take out the stumps
but you can't do that or you don't make anything
and you can't burn 'em cuz the smoke'd give you away
so what you do is you dig a big kind of a pit
and you push 'em all in there good and tight
then you cover over 'em all smooth like
and pray it don't rain to beat hell
over night before the Forest Service inspector
comes along cuz if it does
they'll be there tops shining big and round
as the morning moon and that happened one time
guy comes up from Priest Lake and it'd
rained and the stumps was clear as can be
but if it stays dry you're fine
cuz those guys are allergic to gettin' outta the truck
so long as everything's smoothed kinda over
they can't tell nothing.
                              So Ligans is pushin' a layer over
this pit of stumps and he's backing up the hill
and I knock my Thermos over and it gets to rollin'
and rolls right right under the tread
a D-7 Cat right over the thing
I mean the entire tread goes over it
and I pick it up outta the dirt
and the only thing's wrong with it's the handle's broke off
but when I get down Mary cuz she
won't even throw out the white bread's

got the lifetime warranty in her stack of warranties
in the kitchen drawer and she sends it in
leaving to the side the whole episode with the D-7
and they send it back this new handle strapped on
same as to this day and that was 1974.

## Pitch

No one in Clark Fork, Idaho, mistakes endurance for
the palomino stagnant in his cottonwood swamp
of camper shells and black plastic.
The first university's a hundred miles away.

Pickups cluster their empty cattle and ladder racks
around the Chevron of realistic expectations
as loads of subalpine spruce roll downshifting testimonials
from the furthest edge of elevation.

The wood's lowgrade. But the chainsaws sing from the hills
a full-throated song of omnivorousness. The timbered slope
rises steep as night from the edge of town. Tin roofs.
Dead fireweed. Deer-fenced gardens. Night itself comes in
        gray.

There is so much for us to give ourselves again when
we are weary to descend the switchbacks.
So much to take when we see headlights
high and tiny on the mountain.

Meanwhile the grizzly is stone to the stove smoke smell
of it all. She cannot curse. Vagrant heart,
she pushes her fat shoulders higher
into the last of what we haven't taken.

# Getting Further from the Idaho Line

My father hasn't seen this end of Sanders County
since before I was born.

These windshields of timber and otherwise articulate crags
say nothing of him and his voice isn't
in the occasional tick of pebble in fender.
I've listened.          But what was I hoping to hear?
He'll have long since forgotten this road

and the pink evening silver in the river,
the teeth of eternally black rooted stumps at the bow
ten miles east of Wild Horse Plains.
He'll have forgotten everything but what could
have been the Pair a Dice Bar and sweeping
its table of all but the eight ball, then that
and a railroader's bills counted out on felt.

If it were his words I'm wandering after
I could have called him collect from the booth in Noxon
and he'd have told me how he saw need
rising in steep slopes from the edge
of snowed-under pasture for work and paychecks home.

I'd like to make a lot out of him
pulling lumber that summer on the Libby mill green chain.
But he was back in school by January
and off the farm for good at twenty-one.
That absence is a story these canyons
of afternoon can tell.  One I'm finally glad to hear

that ends with me able to say *timber's impermanence,*
his student loans all paid off, me back here,
him far, both of us knowing
you can't sing to the land if it kills you.

## After I Left

Into some train town we descended,
gates dropping their red-winged warnings
against the steel of redemption
past so much broken glass and back lot plaster, so much
for the religion of Where Have You Gone.
Night thought you up.  We'd killed no one.
Was it '90 or '91?  I woke to floodlights
flooding us, the obedient spin spin atop cop cars
lining up the interrogation,
my face against cold glass, thief in the night
long gone, wreck some voice said
we'd slugged half a mile
miles behind him, the forgiving
thing you'd have thought
tracking through woods, through
the night's wet leaves,
never finding anyone.

## Parole

*"With what delight could I have walked thee round . . . "*
—Milton (*P.L.* IX, 114)

A blowtorch sun glazes the snow in the woods
and his tires sigh a constant, low flame
over dry pavement.  An hour ahead
he'll top the rise over his city,
and he knows he'll want to cut only
the engine, pull to the roadside and sit,
loving as if he'd made it.  That cherished
lake will open, an abscess slit
across the horizon.  The archipelago
will still be iced in, though the icebreaker
arrives with its bruised flags around this time
each year.  He can almost imagine
his impulse ending there, town below
a darling from whom no heartlessness
could exile him.  Houses from that far
are eager and forgivable, the world just physical
and penny-whistle clear.  If, unrecognized,
he could walk those streets, he swears he'd pass
every open window and speak only to the transformers,
angels themselves, humming from high
poles. If the citizens would let him stay
he'd love them for it, he'd stroke their doors
with his empty hand and walk on
into more night.  But they won't have him.
They take the days for themselves only
and would scour the dark to be rid of him.
And so his cruise stays set as his stare,
and the stranded train rusts beside him.
The near trees turn, chorus-line quick
as he passes.  The far trees stand the ridge
like cavalry.  And when the sign says 47 miles
he pictures how, beyond the harbor, seemingly
above it all, the breakwater unbends itself
like his straight razor.

## Night Bicycle

Black mamba of the front tire
over wet streets, the wet streets,
after-rain falling from the neighborhood leaves,
luminescence of lampposts' lamps up
through the trees.

Sink into someone's porch chair
and look at all these leaves
then ride on into the smell of sawdust.
That sweet smell of wood.
Someone is renovating.

May he do it right!
May he be careful.
May he do it right.
May the work of hands satisfy.
Sleep on, Amigos!

The girl who left years ago
loved you behind that window.
She is now some person
living a state away.
Which only makes her more.

You and me, little poem.
Mi amigo.  Compadre.
Inside each dark house
the streetlights keep
doing their thing on the far wall.

Tonight though.  Tonight's
streetlight makes me need you.
It's writing indifference,

36

little poem, indifference
to us on that far wall.

Black mamba of the front tire
over wet streets, the wet streets,
after-rain falling from the neighborhood leaves,
luminescence of lampposts' lamps up
through the trees.

## Geological Proportions

Over the landscape of paper-dry lichen
living on granite at the end of my face

comes the *beep* and *beep* and *beep* and *beep* of a bulldozer
somewhere far off and invisible, call coming in

from clutter, busy signal of saplings
twisting in mud under his treads. And then it stops.

And then I imagine the pitch-green smell crushed
from balsam needles. That's not exactly an objection,

I know. But the world wants inside us the way I want
to nap in sunlight, half asleep and unfurled, cheek

on warm Canadian Shield rock in the cold summit wind.
Here, what we call want is wind tilting a turkey vulture

over the shudder roll of jackpine and birch
five hundred feet beneath me. Here, what we call world

is the sightline from my eye tracing the shadow
of this mountain rising from the bay

to an ore freighter fifteen miles out on Superior.
Why do I belong only to what I abandon?

The highway hidden under forest canopy,
the trail from the highway here where

miles of hills erase their given names
to the horizon, all in the ungovernable down there

will take me back. I'll return fever broken and misfit
as in childhood from my geological proportions,

when the distance to my hand had been a canyon
Piper Cubs could fly through almost unnoticed,

vale a soul could descend into to unmake itself
in the shadows of half-domes as mist rises from a silvery river.

Wilderness is the life we've left,
and any moment's an adequate definition of a life.

If the afternoon can die and this oldest exposed rock
in the world go back down into the inconceivable
       underground,

why shouldn't we?  Here above the numbered ache
to go on, I am a little what I admire

in mountain, the way mountain takes sun.  See how
altitude makes of this forest a blossoming orchard of longings.

III

## American Ballad

*(Josephine Sarah Marcus Earp, 1861 - 1944)*


September, sunset from the deck of the *Governor Pingree* tied
    up for the night,
silt milk gold of the Yukon blushing like a lusty adolescent
    runaway
running away with their fortune.

They'll never make Dawson.
The river will be frozen soon.  But the runaway was her
    anyway
years ago coming into Tombstone.
That violence was brief and it's long gone,
and so went the racehorses, the Colorado meadow and the
    Coeur d'Alene.
Her parents in San Francisco go on
unfolding her letters in the parlor and Wyatt's less prospector
    and lawman
now that he's bankrolled a few mine-town saloons.

The river's gone lead
but the gold in Josie's arctic sky
goes on a long time.

How can the aspen leaves turn
when this vast remote air is so warm
and water drips silky promises
from the sternwheel's still paddles?

They wouldn't be here but she lost the second baby.
After that they abandoned the farm in Wyatt's head
for the novelty of young maps in which so much waits to be
    named
and every new river bend is fullborn
as lamplight spilling from the galley to their feet.

She's thirty-seven.  From the far bank's low, borderless brush
the moon unmoors itself as if made for this,
as if the last green of dusk were a fate it drifted into.
Wyatt holds her hand in that old touching before beauty.

They stare into a future asking nothing of them,
a fever breaking in the aurora,
breaths they can see
when they turn to go in.

They sleep like the children they'll never have.
Frost whitens the stunted trees by dawn.

*

Moonlight's enough to tell weed from onion
and when Josie climbs the ladder she finds Wyatt kneeling,
fingers pinching the dirt for roots
that would claim the cabin's roof garden.
She imagines the dirt in his fingers is warm,
warmed by the day's sun
and the evening fire in the cabin.

The earth on the ground's still frozen
though the Yukon's broke open and the *Governor Pingree* has
        paddled on to Dawson.

When the river iced in eight months ago they were this far,
Rampart, where the Earp name meant something
as it had in every boomtown.
Wyatt found friends and his friends found this home,
a brookside cabin chinked with moss
where he built a spruce-pole bed strung with rope for springs.
Josie spread fur robes for a mattress
and hung calico for curtains.

He hasn't heard her yet over the melt-swollen brook,
so she watches him from the ladder.  He's fifty-one, but lean,
bent like Adam on the shallow slope of what he must remake,
or a nurse, it occurs to Josie, tending
the sprouts of onion and radish and lettuce while she slept on,
        as if, as if. . . .

Well, what's done is done.
Better to think of his silhouette as Noah, the cabin come to rest
        on Mt. Ararat,
the bush all around as ocean receding again.

*

Clouds build a skyline southwest of camp
and lift sand into a yellow wall twenty years taller than
        Tombstone.
Arizona again.  Though they keep *that* town's horizon horizons
        away.
Beyond the far side of another century.
They keep themselves the desert's population.

Josie's no more versed in Torah
than any other Jewish girl from a middle-class family come
        west out of Brooklyn.
Hers is a joy and reverence that sparkles up from silt.
She prays informally, speaking from her bed to her mother's
        Lieber Gott in every desert night.

They've come to this vista after sampling rock for ore all winter
        again,
their second back from Alaska,
and scanning for forage and waterholes
when they topped each ridge—thinking ranch, maybe,

especially when they topped this one.
The money they made selling the Dexter Saloon in Nome's
taken need from the equation.

Between camp and the storm, Wyatt and Josie's horses graze
the far side of the valley
in a painting she's seen, painted high on the wall of a western
train station,
an expanse that seems empty even with figures moving
through,
designed to feel roofless, unfillable, the ceiling full of afternoon
stars,
the desert's red geology dwarfing those little horses.
Thunderheads rise into an empire of sky.

Lightning.  The air's still dry.
This may be home.
Their trial wells opened like pores under the sun
and if one or two of them produce they'll file on the land.
Wyatt's brother Jim has come and the three
have overstayed their plan to be in Los Angeles before the heat
of July
now pushing this storm's first breeze over them.

Jim trots off to move the horses to higher ground.
Wyatt places stones on the tent stakes
and ducks inside to Josie.  He lights a pipe and they watch
from the flap.
"Doesn't all that noise scare you?"
"You'll never hear the thunder from the lightning that gets
you."

\*

When the storm's over there's just warm, constant rain,
roar of water in the gulch and reassurance
in the smell of wet creosote bushes—
that spicy pungency Josie loves.
She thinks of the desert as hers again.

They walk the bank calling across for Jim,
scanning the flood's far side till they spot him
twenty feet up on a cottonwood limb.
Wyatt's holler has the tone of a grin,
"You got the horses up there with you?"
"Not so's you can notice," Jim shouts back.  He's sixty-two.

*

Autumn and Josie steps off the river boat from Yuma
where she'd gotten off the Los Angeles train.
She takes off her hat and lets
her graying black hair take the heat of the sun again.

In the wagon Wyatt says he's built her a house.
He still doesn't know if they'll take up on that land,
but she'll be safe from snakes as long as they last.
"A house?  Really?"

At camp—no building in sight—Wyatt takes Josie's hand,
leads her down to a big mesquite.
Up just into the leaves
a shelter of packing boxes and wagon canvas sits snug
where the huge trunk divides into limbs.
"It's beautiful.  Let's go in."

*

Two days of desert driving from their cottage in Vidal
and they're still a couple miles short of their friend's ranch in
        Indio.
They're in their dusters and scarves,
wearing their goggles and caps when

the momentum of thirty miles per hour
pitches Josie forward and to the side opposite his swing of the
        wheel
when Wyatt tries to miss the bull she screams is in the road.

He's mad. Rushing toward what he's never seen
that's slowing    slowing    swerving almost stopped
                                        *afraid!*
when he lowers his horns and bashes his head
into the radiator. The jolt sends Josie to the floor.
Then she's up. The bull's backing and shaking his lowered
        head,
tossing those horns to warn this enemy
he'll hit him again if need be.
But the car's not moving.

Wyatt reaches into the back seat for the six-shooter shoved
        down among the luggage
and fires a shot in the air. He's seventy.

The bull snorts. A line of silvery mucus and blood dangles
        from one nostril
and trails in the dust as he circles to square up at Josie's side of
        the car.

All she knows of the shootings on Freemont forty years ago
is the sound of the shots, running,

a lull and more shooting, running
and rounding the corner to see the wounded loaded in a
        wagon,
the dead on the ground—and who was standing?

This, and that the O.K. was actually several doors up the street.
The rest she's made from language.

Which is most of any marriage and all of every poem.
                              But here there's also that
tick    tick    tick
while we wait for the bull to rush toward Josie's scream,
for the revolver to find its voice,
for the only thing she's ever seen shot
and the heart to decide,
for the souls of unborn children to inhabit birds,
for the wind to flip its pages,
and for our arrival at the selves we seek
for as long as we all shall live.

IV

## She of Tioga Creek

Marsh went mostly unnoticed then,
and the sun's tremolo through spruce shadows
was just the context our desire used for
your feet on the dash, and the outpost houses
with their dead Chevys were mere residences
for the dusk behind what we decided to say,
and we were never the land we imagined ourselves,
so there's nothing of us to notice now, as I pass.
Not even in the roadside park where we pulled off
and walked the creek up to a dark we used
to unfasten each other from weeks of expectation
in so many other grasses under your back
and where I held the source of your true voice
that, soft, almost mourning, was also the delicate water
inches from your hair where I don't stop
but drive by, past more bleached, dead cedars
we must have passed when we got back on the road
but wouldn't have seen in the night beyond our headlights'
        periphery.

## Three Cafés


Someone, Pietro, somewhere, in Italy,
with his own sense of leisure, Pinot Noir,
and articulation, sketchbook, sits outside at a café
he thinks of as his, that spot in creation
where wind sends its cool breeze
across his loose shirt without riffling his pages.

He thinks no other light gives like this light and
of course he's right.
                    As is Antonio
who sees it as lonely, in another district
of the same small city, at his own café,
getting right the widow's monologue
in his new play while pigeons watch
and the fountain gurgles away.  Pietro and Antonio
have never met, though they'd recognize
each other, being of an age, late twenties,
and both spending so much time alone in public
the last couple years—the cinema, walking
the road lined with Lombardy poplars
beside the bay, the market every Saturday.

Pietro buys bananas; Antonio bread.
Pietro rents a room; Antonio's father is dead.

He lives at home with his mother
and seventeen-year-old sister, Nicoletta, with whom
he's worked to stay close.  Evenings,
at the kitchen table, they often play chess.
Their mother does the dinner dishes.
Their father had a policy, so Antonio

needn't work.  He should write, his mother insists,
and stay home for Nico (though soon she'll
be off to Parma for University).

Pietro tacks his sketches, the few he likes,
to the wall in his room.  His favorite
is of two girls on bikes.  The first girl
glances over her shoulder at the other
behind her, that sunny wind he knows so well
in her hair.
            And meanwhile here, at my café,
countries, an ocean, and states away, I imagine
her riding past him, and in my own
sun and leisure and new love of Pietro and Antonio
consider whether she should be Nico
or some other girl, someone none of us knows.

## Influence

Halliday's in Italy and Koch is dead
(though I admit Koch never meant much to me).
What matters is he made Halliday feel understood
in (I imagine) much the way Halliday made me.
I read him and knew I was free.
A few years later he read me
and just often enough responded enthusiastically
(all the more shining as he's so known for being curmudgeonly.
At least when it comes to poems. The opposite's true of his
        company.)

Writing poems is lonely.
At its best at least it has almost nothing to do with loyalty.
But today I'm sad for Halliday
and the new way he's on his own.
Far from home. A rolling stone. And
(as far as Koch's concerned) a complete unknown.

## University Surplus

I don't want to be here
   to think of all the sex
in the six-foot stack
   of spent dorm mattresses,
a dollar apiece,

or the years of eyes
   that strained for some glimmer
of understanding just beyond
   these computer screens, as blank
in rows on folding tables

as night after night
   of overcast above
the observatory, where
   someone waited to show
what he knew of eternity.

There's too much importance,
   too much of you and me
out among the sunlit benches,
   library steps and hedges
of today to stay

sifting racks of warm-up pants
   for a pair my size
and running my fingers
   over the coffee circle stained
veneer of someone's desk

who also spent some days
   at the sunlit pinnacle
of history, doing

serious work, no doubt,
wholly in the moment

once in a while—
   the smell of coffee,
solidity of this desk
   and beautiful thoughts
no one's bothered to salvage.

# Bones in the River

*for Dan Morris*

Here is your narrative
and your narrative place,
a confusion of elk bones
amber through amber melt water
and drawn out along the silt bed
bow of Slough Creek.  Friend,
what besides hunger invents
the world, snow and rock toothed
mandible of the Absaroka, parabola
of a hundred million spruce needles
sloping to end in this valley
floor of close grasses for the elk,
the elk for the wolves?
Downstream, in the narrows
before the falls, where the weight
of water first pulls the taut surface
into a thigh flexed in the shadow
of sheer rock and the low air
smells wet and cool, the river
parts for a boulder.  There the owl
stood on his talons, neither threat
nor threatened, to cough up
a molecule the size of a woman's thumb.
Even balled firm dry fur and tiny claws
weigh less than you imagine.
Hold it in the hollow of your
hand.  When you are ready
to begin your earth will need
a heart for its first lover.

## The Spotting Scope

The dead do not rise, unless you count
the flesh scheduled to ascend in the guts
of a golden eagle and how many crows
once the eagle manages to dig its way through
fur and skin. The wolf, a young female
bedded with her pack this morning's now
flat on her side in the snow. Her pack
and the pack that ran her down and bit her
and bit her, tails wagging in the air till she died,
are both miles from here. This morning:
sun, a couple turns and flopping down
with a drowsy sigh. Now: the eagle
adjusting its stance, flexing its talons
in her fur, wind that doesn't mean anything.
No. My four-year-old has no questions. She looks
but not long. Soon she's back to her stick
where the snow's receded, working the mandible
of an elk loose from the frozen ground.

## Fire Season

This haze that was just yesterday bark and needle and
        dry-frond fern
a hundred and fifty-some miles west of here has dulled the
        windbreak of Lombardy poplars
and the field of cut hay in round bails as surely as centuries
        mute paint.
Neither landscape nor representation, we don't dim or flame
        out,
but people who loved me my whole life have died and they
        too have taken a brightness with them.

I still address the air.  The heart's still answered by the breeze
until the day ends, heat lightning on wheat fields, dry clouds
        and the flight patterns of tiny lights
lining up on approach, coming in from the side of the sky
        that's still stars.
It all seems so clear, and in the morning color returns.
But smell that?  And look beyond the middle distance:

Those molecules were forest so long it's as if they don't know
what to do with themselves now but haunt the senses of those
        who were never there
when it was cool and clouds moved through when the rain
        was done.
I should have expected this.  It's an old song, *Whither is fled the
        visionary gleam?*
fire season in the Cascades and *smoke gets in your eyes.*

Once I stood below the cleaning of the Sistine Chapel and, my
        God!
behind the scaffold moving a few feet a year, those were the
        colors

of a younger world, of a living Michelangelo, and time was
        merely the soot
from a million hours of candles, to be tenderly brushed away
        from true blue,
first green of creation, our skin as if lit from within.

You can't tell me the world wasn't meant to be that bright.
I remember the air we all lived in.
When I go to the forest I know, sun over the mountain ticks the
        tin roof warm again.
This smoke will clear. One clean autumn day waits, vivid and
        restored,
and the light will be almost enough to believe I am loved like
        that again.

## Brave Coast, No Wheels

In the infinite divisibility of a moment—
say, the park woods
in the sun of a June day in 1996,
my father with a stick,
he and my mother and I in sweatshirts
because of the chill breeze still
coming in off Lake Superior,
the three of us strolling, my father
swinging his stick through
the trailside grass, my hands
behind my back, my mother
noticing the translucence of the young leaves
just above us—is the implication
that we can live forever there.
Maybe. Maybe. But when I look up
what I see makes me think of Troy (seriously),
long wall along the promontory rim
and ramparts shadowing the beach.
My wife and daughter are beachcombing there
and though that is the Mediterranean
this is not Ionia, it's northeastern Spain.
Still, the fortification towers right there,
from which wives and parents
could look down on the sand
and even plead for a husband
and son to come inside. Please,
come inside. The day of the first dialysis
she missed, my mother came up
to speak over her morphine,
lifted her eyelids just to the pupil
and that very specific green
and said, "The days have no wheels."
There's a cartload of medical history,

toes and then toes and then feet,
fingers to knuckle, knuckle to hand,
long, long division of years
since that park walk in the sun.
There was also fun. My daughter was born.
Some picnics. A seagull pivoting his head
to see our sandwiches with his other eye.
Days that had wheels where once they had feet.
Zeno lied (or at least got it wrong):
look around. Slice it down enough and that June day dies,
the present gets in through the gate,
we even celebrate (I mean, here
we are, in Spain!). Anya brings me
a stick from the beach
and I tell her gracias. But
a breeze blew through the woods.
It smelled clean and cold like the lake.
My mother zipped up her sweatshirt.

V

## Perspective Unrecovered

I lost the poem that got right
that thing that happens
when, walking or driving by, you look
in the front window of a house
and see through to and out a window
in back.  It had things like
leaded glass in there, the framed leaves
on the tree in the backyard,
and the house was a specific,
powder-blue house at Third and College,
and, most importantly, reading the poem
I was sure that people would know
the kind of moment I was after,
a moment in which you inhabit the house
and (sort of) those who must live there
and look out that back window, all the while
remaining yourself very much outside
in the summer sun on Third Street,
walking by.  There was other stuff
I've forgotten about, a harbor and kites,
but since the poem's been lost
I've allowed myself the indulgence
of thinking of that front to back window
passage as *significant*, a metaphorical
construct with *resonance*, a *complexity*
that kept it right at the edge of articulable,
the variables realigning and turning like light
splashing open through the prisms
of that beveled glass into tiny spectrums
moving through the room all afternoon—
poem, house, Third Street, poet, backyard, reader,

glass, the imagined temperature of air inside,
the air on your skin. I *absolutely* do not claim
that this poem achieves the level of human connection
(I think) that one did. That one bet everything
on the experience itself. If you'd read it
you'd feel what it was to stand there,
sun on the skin of your arms, the same
sun on those backyard leaves through both windows.
But then, you've lost things, too. You know.

# The Word "Curl"

To the cargo of that vast old vessel, my lifetime
has added Art Garfunkel's hair,

so that now, amid the billions of possible associations—
woodshavings, tapeworms, old fingers, and speaker wire—

we've got Garfunkel, above and behind Simon
on the cover of *Bridge Over Troubled Water*,

hair rising like a single, boiling thunderhead
over what must have been two extremely alive young men,

hair hanging a little dismissively loose, like Dylan's then too,
I suppose, hair that had already gone everywhere,

so that when, in a new century, I see my student,
lanky and twenty and walking down the street in a world

completely with him, I can tell you
about the curl in his hair

and we'll have the comfort of knowing together
he is beautiful in a way that returns.

## Tend

The orphan window washer is an old man in a driver's cap
walking the cold August street of his self-appointed day off.

Town raised him, little hills of houses, long curve of the bay,
the cathedral every Wednesday and Sunday,

so he tends town's flowers, weeding the pocket gardens,
and pulls his squeegee down every self-portrait on town's
        main drag.

We're better among.  Flying over or considering town as
        analogy
reduces us, but even the window washer can't help himself
        sometimes.

He'll start here tomorrow—a storefront with no awning.
In the glass he's large but it's over his shoulder

he looks as he does often, beyond gables,
to the town's trees and their seasons,

their height, their approval,
dust in the pattern of last night's rain.

## Flanigan's Pen

I just hold the pen. I'm a Christian.
The words ain't me.
In rehab I wrote and sent it to those guys
who wrote the Big Book. They said send it
somewhere else cuz it's crazy shit.
Before that was Beirut, '80-'89, Baby.
Love them B52s. 3000 mph. Bye!
B52s, my man, turns sand to glass. Bye!
I don't hang out. I got this land
out in Forestville. A guy's gonna leave it to me.
I camp there but last night I slept at the laundry.
Do you know Leadbelly?
Sometimes I stay in the country.
Sometimes I stay in town.
Sometimes I get a great notion
to jump in the river and drown.
You can call my name but I walk 3000 mph
with my nose to the ground.
I'm gonna take a little punch.                    Mmm.
Mmm. You gotta carry in your pocket these days.
I just write it down. It's a text,
know what I'm sayin'? No fuckin' book.
A text. You study it. You don't fuckin' read it.
You ain't gonna get what it means, man.
Not a text. You wanna read read a book.
Mo Fo.          Read a book!
Know what I'm sayin'? Yeah you do.
But I don't hang out. Except Flanigan's.
How you like that? Flanigan in Flanigan's.
Fuckin' seals send a wingnut down 90 ft
40 lbs each ankle no watch how much air?
See if they can kill a wingnut. Octopus moving
over coral the color of your own brain

an `cutas turnin' like 16s off the deck.
Up past my land's where that guy Nick's got his cabin
huge fuckin' logs and bears and eagles all over the place.
Nick can do anything with a chainsaw.
But it's the same thing.  You think he does that?
You think that chainsaw's him?  I been to Vegas.
I been all over and that Chainsaw ain't him.
Nagano, Japan.  CBS Sports my man.
They ain't playin'.  They're just the cameras.
Ask the bobsled what it means.
I love dogs.  It's people I can't stand.
I smoke cigars and I'm in Flanigan's
and he says my wife don't like those
so I say why they don't vibrate?
and he says she don't want cigar smokin' in here.
Tell her to go to church, I say.
Why don't you just put it out? he says.
So I grabbed his hair and put it out in his eye.
Shhh. . . . You ain't buyin' it?  Look here Jack
under my hat.  How about that?
How about that three-way?  Sweet!
Peeled it right to the bone with a beer mug.
I stopped cuz I seen your books
and seen you here writin'.     Here.
Here you go.  Here's the pen.

## Third Street and the Stolen Boat

Lampposts tattoo the short shadows of objectivity onto
        concrete.
Luminescence pierces the lip of every overhanging leaf.

The last of August, sunlit chill breeze and constant sparkle of
        university traffic again.
A skateboard double clacks the coronary insistence of
        adolescence

under a whiff of curry from some apartment or other
and past the toe heel arch kicks of three guys hacky-sacking
        outside Wicked Ink.

What the day defies isn't so much season
(though the air's so clear I can see fall four blocks north at
        Prospect),

as the formlessness of any dying.  After all,
isn't all this for us, whether offered or found?

Like the little dull aluminum cloud of winter the boy spots
stashed in the shore brush where some ice fisherman must
        have left it,

insurance against rotten ice, to push out over the surface of
        another pushed season.
If boats believed, it wouldn't believe what's being expected of it:

to float.  But it floats and the boy stands
gondolier-poling the sandy lake bottom with a driftwood
        cedar pole.

Sunset adds its radiance to weeks of sun in his skin.
There are no oars but wind chops the water,

and now the pole finds nothing down there.
Trees are as small as the aftermath of make-believe.

He plunges a hand into the cold glove of Superior and paddles
but the dark band of shore continues to shorten.

Headlights glisten from the stretch he knows
is miles up the coast where highway edges the beach.

Then the yellow lights of a few homes line up their bon voyage
for him to shout himself hoarse into

until they're a failed, fallen constellation under the dimmer
but more certain stars, running lights of indifference's endless
      navy,

a launched armada of escorts into unmappable absence.
Back in town, back in the neighborhood of the only star

we imagine fixes us, a boy I know parades his scarf-draped
      boa
Pandora up to my sidewalk table and my time

de-rasaing another tabula without touching the scene is done.
The snake's a river-vine sheen twining herself

around him with slow deliberation, docile as marble
warm in the sun under my hand.  Her eye is watching me.

It's the eye of the emissary from this moment's garden.
*Come in, come in, it's all been written.*

Wind flips a few yellow pages and riffles them
but they're nothing as yellow as the quivering, window-box
      snapdragons

swaying as though charmed by the ordinary music
of slow traffic in the poem wind makes of afternoon.

Wither's working its brown way up, leaf to leaf,
but their stems are long.  Their bloom-yellow fever

won't be broken today.  Nor will the moon rising at the lake's
        horizon
on that other boy, the boat on a sand bar waves lift him off

and set him back on again.  How deep's the water,
how far the swim to the dark cliffs of that island?

Little tosses of wave tip spill in     spill in     spill in.
His Adidas are soaked so he bails his heart out with one

till the waves work him free and he's spent.
He doesn't drift toward the island,

though he sees the top of every pine's outline
as it passes in front of the moon.

The plank seat's wide enough for him to curl to sleep on
and he sleeps, supposing the long walk to a phone

from wherever he'll land, his eventual bed,
and only for breath-seizing instants the vertigo of blackness

to the lakefloor deepening away from him.

## Leave and the Dream of This Street Starts Over

Still, it's a pleasant dream—citizens walk the sidewalk
talking, taking your place, the taste of beer,
conversations ascending finch-like in the low air.
But look instead (while you can) at what's here
that does not close behind any of us when we go,
forgettable details, fluting up the lamppost
and three shades of cream brick and chrome framing
the shop window and ferns fireworking
from buckets hung beneath the awning and the awning
and ripples cool air makes moving over these.
A noun weighs exactly nothing
and neither does a day. But that's a trade
worth taking. (Take the day!) Though once you're gone
the poem will seem to say otherwise.
Next time you're here the sky'll be a mess of snow
so snow is the atmosphere to imagine
despite the current sun, late and low, sharpening
every saber of grass in the yard across the street
to the sheen of plucked-string high notes
coming out the propped-open tavern door.
The local Jim Morrison's hair's gone gray.
He holds his own wife's hand into the funeral home.
And the campus radio host walks eating ice cream
two spoonfuls per block from a Coca Cola cup.
Enjoy. Enjoy. Forget snow. Girls flip their flip-
flops by. The stars are yet unseen.
Another half-hour of long shadow to go.

VI

# Detail

But what if emotion's not all that contingent on the specifics of
        situation—
skirt, her Converse All Stars, the names of that bar and the
        cover band,
your name + "you're the one"?

And what about home?  Dixon, Patterson, Marquette.
Don't we reside in
little waves the breeze makes along the café awning?
Our reflections off storefront glass framed in the familiarity of
        old chrome?
The red and white seersucker hat that three-year-old wears
        walking her mother up the sidewalk's a closer
        approximation
as they approach your usual table.                Her grin.

## Daughter

In the sling back chair, under wind
in white pines that will outlast us both,
breaths filled our lungs for free
and we returned them as freely.
Your back rose and fell as you rode
the slower waves of my chest.
Little lifeboat, tiny astronaut, your eyes
under lids read dreams
I imagined only by staring skyward
to those trees sweeping arcs again
and again across that space where they end
and beyond them begins and clouds
scrolling above.  What I knew then
was this: there is no stillness and never was.

# In

Sometimes I'd leave the flashlight
knowing it meant walking the dark ten minutes
back from the barn by the overhead break
in fir and pine, feet staying to the invisible
scuff of dirt in the road's left rut.
How many moonless nights
in dark canyons of forest remained
before the sky was to close over sensation?
No one knows, sure, but fewer now than then.
The dog barked out the cabin's position.
From further than you'd think
he could hear my footfalls.
He quieted when I called out to him.
*Good dog* I've said over and over,
my mouth to his ear giving him something
he might follow one last time.  And now he's buried
in a woods way back in Michigan
while I hold the T.V. remote as far into night
as sleep holds out, keeping the room
awash in antipoetic illumination
that glows on after I'm gone down
into my dream shoveling dirt and crumbly sandstone,
his side giving a little as the weight falls
on the blanket we've wrapped him in.
Living human years as I do I'm still young, relatively,
and the patience of the woods is legendary.
Odds are I'll walk the dark in Idaho again.
But no one else knew Odysseus,
home after twenty years, except the dog
who recognized his passing voice
and so died satisfied.  At least
someone thought so.  Are we who we were once
and then never again?  Labor Day comes

with clouds closing and I'm parked
at the end of a long curve of bay.
A half-dozen people knee-deep in the pewter riffles
of Superior under pewter sky. Everyone else on shore.
It went about how I'd expected, except
for the shaved square of skin on his foreleg
and the size of the syringe, how much thick, pink liquid
there was, and how it seemed to hurt some
going in. His muscles tensed.
We had to hurry with our reassurances.
Which brings me to what I've left out:
Amy, on her knees on the ground beside me
as I spoke in his ear and stroked his fur,
pushing my shoulder gently so she could see
his eyes. Which saw her. Which never closed.
The fiction of narrative solitude is the poet's old lie,
and most of us do it and those who do know why. After all,
there's no one else here now, on this near isthmus of memory.
Though it's less than he'd have perceived
from the seat behind me, the smell
through these open windows today
is everything another year has made
smelling crushed full of pine, cloud thick and leafy.
Some days there's more to do.
Some days it seems it's all been done.
So if I'm to be my own key witness and unwavering
company I'll look out as though it's in
where the still warm breeze moves the limbs
of trees turned and determined by a lifetime
of wind, until the waders all come in, rain
draws its curtain halfway across the horizon,
and the iron freighter arriving
passes the iron freighter going away.

## None of This Is Saying Goodbye

The deaths of everyone you love ask nothing.
Outwant the new choir of stars.
Slide back the sunroof
or even the sun. Sing
over the wind lifting your hair
or accelerate a little over the rise so
the highway seems to fall away
from you like a runway while
a new horizon of prairie hangs itself
in the long gallery of your day.
You won't worry anyone loose of the end.
Not yourself. Not her. Not him.
You're free to pass the truckstop pay phone
free not to pull to the side miles later
free not to step out into dusk sage air.
You don't even have to notice the absence
of others on this road nor the teal western sky
nor the fence posts' insistence
in their diminishing capital I.

## Resolve

Boiling with worry, he went out into the day even when it was
    sunny.
*Please release me, circumstances,* he'd pray,
*and keep my loves safe on the curb from every head-crushing tire.*
*Kill the bacteria before it can breed.*
*Walk the killer on past their doors, blade folded in his pocket.*
*O let their lab results come back baseline.*
*Protect them.*
He promised he'd appreciate the trees, inspect them for new
    life
and lift his eyes to the music of rows of old houses,
snow baking on the black-shingled roof of every porch,
he'd walk with hands in his pockets and a happy sigh
for the morning and those in it, passing slowly in unwashed
    cars that glimmer a little anyway,
he'd remember that somewhere some were in *actual* agony,
every comfort denied them by design,
he'd be grateful and kind at every random encounter—eye
    contact and at least a smile and nod,
he'd look forward to lunch, another meal for him in this life of
    abundance,
he'd forgive his enemies,
and he'd ask forgiveness for all he'd missed while imagining
    the torch someone could touch to his bright fields of
    affection,
if only he could be given some reassurance,
a sign that they, those who knew what goodness he was
    capable of when unafraid,
would go on.

## Morning in a New Year

Those streetlights are no wiser going off
than they were coming on.

Under a brightening, featureless overcast,
town is a great liner washed up on its own shore.

The antennae no one's bothered to take down
go right on receiving.

This is not the brain's town, where we can be remembered,
but the one with clapboard we could peel

to framewood no one alive's ever seen.
On the other Northern Hemisphere it's also winter.

The old poet has had a stroke and lives,
citizen of a land with no word for spruce.

He's one soul among many.  But then, so are we.
When we hear that he holds and holds his wife's hand

he teaches us a language we will need,
in a dialect from where bare trees touch

above our roofs and under our ground.

## Teleological North:  Year's End


All along the coast waves rattle pebbles
into caves and out of this disconsolate wind.
No language conceives them, and when they dry
they'll lose their sheen.  There are *people* to love.

A snowman rides by in a pickup bed,
arms spreading benediction behind him,
with a beneficent, stone grin, *fair creature of an hour*, scarf
flapping the motion of moving away.

Street lamps end the afternoon coming on,
and December comes to this, the mute, made things
of a day, lacquered hard in their indifference—

melt wet street, silvery back sides of No Parking signs,
enamel burgundy of a Caravan.  Alone
or not alone, our job remains the same.

## Vango's, Tuesday Night in the
## Week of the Buddha's Enlightenment

*for Paul Lehmberg*

Snow falls. Stress the first syllable.
Not like Vincent van•Gógh's but Ván•go's.
Snow falls. Say it and step out before Jim and Ray
finish "Into the Mystic" so that the guitar follows
even after the door closes behind you to *when that foghorn blows*
*you know I will be coming home* as the rumble
comes rooflight riding the plow up Third
and passes just as Ray finally hits that high note you've waited
       for all night
at *I* . . . to the spark-tossing-thunder of blade on asphalt up
       through your feet into
*want to rock your gypsy soul* to the side-to-side lights on the back
       of the plow
by now passing Crescent and Discount Vacuum, the Pasta
       Shop, Prospect Street.
If a town could take you to bed, this is her touching your cheek
       just before
and you go knowing the music will fill this cold air where you
       were
through three   four   five more passes of the plow
as you sleep and Jim unplugs his bass and the Vango's sign
       goes dark.
Let this be how it is just before dying
knowing what you noticed remains.